SCARY PLACES

Creepy Islands

by Dinah Williams

Consultant: Paul F. Johnston, PhD
Washington, D.C.

BEARPORT
PUBLISHING

New York, New York

Credits

Cover and Title Page, © manu_83/Fotolia, © Manuel Fernandes/Fotolia, © William Berry/Fotolia, and © Galyna Andrushko/Fotolia; 4–5, © Krivosheev Vitaly/Shutterstock, © Simon Dannhauer/Shutterstock, © thanapun/Shutterstock; 6, © Matthews, James Skitt, Major (1878–1970); 7, © BC Government; 8, © Dan Waters; 9, © The Granger Collection, New York / The Granger Collection; 10, © Stephen Saks/Getty Images; 10TR, © Blackbeard (c.1680-1718) (gouache on paper), Hook, Richard (b.1938)/Private Collection/ © Look and Learn/The Bridgeman Art Library; 11T, © John Pineda/Getty Images; 11B, © AP Photo/The News & Observer, Robert Willett; 12, © Peter Randall; 13T, © Aprilphoto/Shutterstock; 13B, © Elisabeth Ansley / Arcangel Images; 14L, © Pictorial Press Ltd / Alamy; 14R, © GeoEye; 15, © Associated Press; 16, © Lindle Markwell/BBC News; 17T, © moodboard/Corbis; 17B, © Meister Photos/Shutterstock; 18, © James N. Scott; 19, © Russell Barber; 20, © Adam Ward / Alamy; 20TR, © courtesy of Gay Baldwin; 21T, © Naturenet/Wikipedia; 21B, © katalinks/Shutterstock; 22, © Courtesy of Prefeitura Municipal Itanhaém; 23T, © Marcio Martins; 23B, © Courtesy of Reptile Gardents/Nitro Images; 24T, © Randy Olson/National Geographic Society/Corbis; 24B, © Johnny Stockshooter / Alamy; 25T, © Alberto Loyo/Shutterstock; 25B, © Tero Hakala/Shutterstock; 26, © NY Daily News Archive via Getty Images; 27, © Arthur Schatz/Time Life Pictures/Getty Images; 31, © kwest/Shutterstock; 32, © Dr. Morley Read/Shutterstock.

Publisher: Kenn Goin
Editorial Director: Adam Siegel
Creative Director: Spencer Brinker
Design: Dawn Beard Creative
Cover: Kim Jones
Photo Researcher: We Research Pictures, LLC

Library of Congress Cataloging-in-Publication Data

Williams, Dinah.
  Creepy islands / by Dinah Williams.
      pages cm. — (Scary places)
  Includes bibliographical references and index.
  ISBN-13: 978-1-62724-294-3 (library binding)
  ISBN-10: 1-62724-294-5 (library binding)
 1. Islands—History—Anecdotes—Juvenile literature. 2. Haunted places—Juvenile literature.
3. Ghosts—Juvenile literature. I. Title.
  BF1461.W5349 2015
  133.10914'2—dc23
                                2014010735

For more information, write to Bearport Publishing Company, Inc., 45 West 21st Street, Suite 3B, New York, New York 10010. Printed in the United States of America.

10 9 8 7 6 5 4 3 2 1

Contents

Creepy Islands

Imagine you've been sailing for weeks, staring out to sea day after day. You are low on supplies and hopelessly lost. Suddenly you spot it—a small island in the distance. As you head toward it, you're nervous about what you'll find.

You have no choice but to go ashore. Beware, however, if you find yourself on one of the islands in this book. For as you continue walking, you might discover a swamp filled with hungry crocodiles, a beach haunted by the ghost of a headless pirate, or a forest filled with trees that have **coffins** hanging from their branches. Welcome ashore!

Coffins in the Trees

Deadman Island, Vancouver, Canada

Today, Deadman Island lies just off the downtown area of Vancouver, a seaport city in western Canada. In the mid-1800s, however, the city had not yet been built. Deadman Island belonged to the Squamish people—**Native Americans** who lived in the area. Their name for the place was a word that simply meant "island." So how did it get its new, much scarier name?

Deadman Island

John Morton was one of Vancouver's first white **settlers**. One day in 1862, he rowed across the water to what is now Deadman Island. When he looked up, he made a shocking discovery. Hundreds of coffins were swaying in the trees. How did they get there?

Native American tree burial coffin

Two hundred Squamish warriors had been killed on the island during a battle between rival tribes. After the battle, the Squamish considered the island "dead ground"—they thought it could be used only for tree burials. In this traditional type of burial, the bodies of the dead are placed in cedar coffins and then tied high up in the trees.

John Morton had been considering purchasing the island. During his visit, however, he poked one of the coffins with a pole. The rotting box broke. Bones and a skull with long black hair rolled out. Not surprisingly, Morton decided not to buy the island.

In the late 1800s, white settlers also used the island to bury their dead. Among them were people who died in Vancouver's Great Fire of 1886, as well as victims of a **smallpox** outbreak that occurred just a few years later. These burials, along with the earlier ones, led to the island's current name.

7

The Lost Colony

Roanoke Island, North Carolina

In July 1587, a group of more than 100 men, women, and children arrived on Roanoke (ROH-uh-nohk) Island, just off the coast of North Carolina. They hoped to make a brand-new life for themselves in a land far from their old homes in England. Yet something very different happened instead. Most of them disappeared without a trace.

Roanoke Island, with a ship that was built to look like the one that brought the settlers from England

The leader of the **colonists** who landed on Roanoke Island was named John White. In August 1587, about a month after the group had landed, he made the difficult decision to sail back to England with some of the men for supplies. White planned to return to the island quickly. The trip to England and back should have taken three months. Due to a war between England and Spain, however, it took more than two years.

When White finally returned in 1590, he found the island **deserted**. The only clue to the missing colonists' whereabouts was the word "Croatoan" (*kroh*-uh-TOH-un) carved in a fence post. This was the name of a local Native American tribe.

White sailed back to England, never learning what had become of the colonists. Some people believe that they split into two groups. One group was killed by hostile Chesapeake Indians, while the other was taken in by friendly Croatoan Indians. These are only **theories**, however. The truth remains a mystery.

The settlers who landed on Roanoke Island in 1587 are known today as "The Lost Colony."

John White discovering the word "Croatoan"

Blackbeard's Revenge

Ocracoke Island, North Carolina

While many pirates roamed the East Coast during the early 1700s, few were as feared as Edward Teach—better known as Blackbeard. Not surprisingly, this dangerous outlaw met with a violent end. His final battle was fought on a small island off the coast of North Carolina. Some say he swims in the waters there still.

Ocracoke Island

Blackbeard

By 1718, Blackbeard was a powerful pirate with a number of ships under his command. In May of that year, his fleet boldly blocked the port of Charleston, South Carolina. Blackbeard and his men then took treasure off any approaching ships. After the **blockade**, Blackbeard retreated to his hideout in a **cove** on Ocracoke Island. There, nearly 200 pirates celebrated for a week.

A few months later, the governor of Virginia decided to take action. He hired a British navy lieutenant named Robert Maynard to arrest Blackbeard. As Maynard's ship approached the cove, Blackbeard responded with cannon fire. Many in Maynard's crew died. The rest hid below deck. When Blackbeard boarded the ship, the hidden men burst from below and attacked. The powerful pirate was shot 5 times and stabbed 25 times before finally dying.

To prove he had caught Blackbeard, Maynard cut off the pirate's head and hung it on the front of his ship. He dumped Blackbeard's body into the cove. Blackbeard's crew claimed that it swam three times around the ship before sinking. Some say his headless ghost has since been seen in the water and on the beaches searching for his head.

A model of Blackbeard's ship the *Queen Anne's Revenge*

In 1996, one of Blackbeard's ships, the *Queen Anne's Revenge*, was found in water about 50 miles (80 km) from Ocracoke Island. On it were many cannons—some fully loaded—as well as thousands of other **artifacts**.

An anchor recovered from the *Queen Anne's Revenge*

Treasure Island

Appledore Island, New Hampshire

In 1703, there were few reasons to visit rocky and deserted Appledore Island off the coast of New Hampshire. One good reason, though, was to hide stolen treasure. John Quelch was said to have done exactly that before he was captured for **piracy**.

Appledore Island

John Quelch was part of a crew hired to catch pirates. In July 1703, the crew's ship, the *Charles*, was ready to set sail from Marblehead, Massachusetts. Quelch and the crew, however, had other plans. They threw the captain overboard, stole the ship, and sailed south. There, the bloodthirsty crew attacked any ship unlucky enough to cross their path. Soon the *Charles* was packed full with stolen goods.

Quelch then did something no one expected. He sailed back to Marblehead. Once there, he began to boldly lie. Quelch claimed the captain wasn't thrown overboard, but had died peacefully at sea. He also said that the treasure on the *Charles* had come from a wrecked Spanish ship. Unfortunately for Quelch, however, his crew told the true story. As a result, in 1704, Quelch was hanged for piracy.

Before returning to Marblehead, Quelch had made one known stop—Appledore Island. There, he was said to have buried nearly 200 pounds (91 kg) of gold and silver, which was never found. Since his death, many people on Appledore have seen the ghost of a pirate. Some think it is the **spirit** of Quelch, looking for his hidden treasure.

Near Appledore Island is White Island. According to **legend**, a Scottish pirate left his sweetheart on the island to guard his treasure. When he failed to return, she died of a broken heart. Her beautiful, golden-haired ghost has since been seen staring out to sea, as if still waiting for her beloved to come back.

Did She Survive?

Nikumaroro Island, Southwest Pacific Ocean

In the spring of 1937, Amelia Earhart began a daring quest to be the first woman to fly around the world. Yet in July, near the end of the trip, her plane disappeared. Or did it? Some say it crash-landed at **remote**, **uninhabited** Nikumaroro Island. If that is true, then what happened to Earhart?

Nikumaroro Island

Amelia Earhart

On July 2, 1937, Amelia Earhart and her **navigator** Fred Noonan took off from New Guinea, a large island in the southwest Pacific Ocean. Their next stop was tiny Howland Island, 18 hours away. Their plane never arrived, however. The U.S. government spent the next 17 days searching an area of 250,000 square miles (647,497 sq km) before giving up. Perhaps, however, the search was called off too soon.

Researchers have spent years trying to piece together what happened. With the help of high-tech equipment, they were able to pinpoint tiny and deserted Nikumaroro Island—350 miles (563 km) southeast of Howland—as the spot where they believe Earhart's plane went down. They also believe that artifacts that have been found on the island over the years—including human bones, parts of a man's and woman's shoes, and the remains of a campsite—suggest that Earhart and Noonan may have been there and survived the crash. Tragically, however, with no fresh water on the island—and no one coming to their rescue—they would have died within a few weeks of **dehydration**.

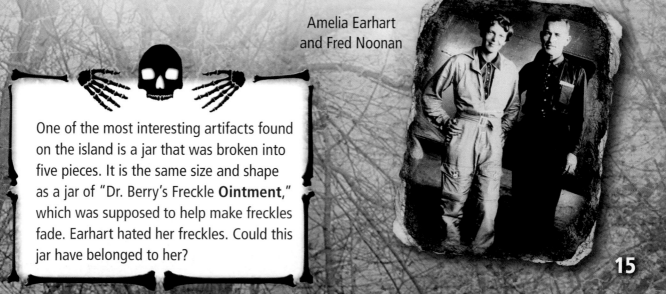

Amelia Earhart and Fred Noonan

One of the most interesting artifacts found on the island is a jar that was broken into five pieces. It is the same size and shape as a jar of "Dr. Berry's Freckle **Ointment**," which was supposed to help make freckles fade. Earhart hated her freckles. Could this jar have belonged to her?

Deadly Swamps

Ramree Island, Myanmar

During World War II (1939–1945), many battles were fought over small islands in the Pacific Ocean. Yet one fight was not among soldiers. Instead, it was a fight between a group of soldiers and nature—and the soldiers lost.

Ramree Island

Ramree is a tiny island off the coast of Burma, a country now known as Myanmar. On January 21, 1945, British forces attacked Japanese soldiers who were camped there. After more than three weeks of fierce fighting, approximately 900 Japanese soldiers planned their **retreat**. Unfortunately, the only place to go was ten miles (16 km) into the island's saltwater swamps.

On the evening of February 19, the Japanese soldiers waded into the waist-high water. They met with poisonous scorpions, **malaria**-infested mosquitoes, and deadly snakes. Yet the worst creatures they faced were the 17-foot-long (5.1 m) saltwater crocodiles. Known to charge out of the water, these giant reptiles snatch and then drown their victims before eating them.

Bruce Stanley Wright, a British soldier who served in the battle, wrote what he heard that night: "Scattered rifle shots . . . and the screams of wounded men crushed in the jaws of huge reptiles." He also reported that only about 20 of the enemy soldiers came out of the swamps alive.

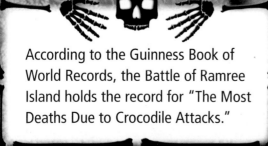

According to the Guinness Book of World Records, the Battle of Ramree Island holds the record for "The Most Deaths Due to Crocodile Attacks."

Terrible Tilly

Tillamook Rock, Oregon

In 1879, an expert **stonemason** named John Trewavas arrived at Tillamook Rock to help build a lighthouse. However, as he tried to land on the tiny, rocky island, a large wave swept him off the boat and out to sea. His body was never found. So began the dark history of the island lighthouse now known as "Terrible Tilly."

Waves crashing on Tillamook Rock

By January 1881, a 62-foot (18.8 m) tower rose from Tillamook Rock. Workers had almost completed the lighthouse that Trewavas had been planning to help build. One foggy night, the workers heard a boat nearing the island's rocky coast. Quickly, they lit a bonfire and placed lanterns in the tower to warn the boat to stay away. It was too late, however. The boat crashed into the rocks and sank, drowning all 16 people on board. The only survivor was the crew's dog.

The lighthouse's **beacon** was lit a few days later, but the weather stayed as rough as ever. Over the years, violent storms repeatedly pounded Tillamook Rock. Waves crashed through the lighthouse windows and flooded the building. Winds reached 109 miles per hour (175 kph), hurling rocks at the lighthouse walls.

Due to the strong wind, crashing waves, and **isolation**, many lighthouse keepers quit. Others were said to have been driven crazy by the loneliness. By 1957, when the lighthouse was closed, it was said that no one would work there. Yet people on the mainland claim to still see ghostly lights beaming from the now-deserted island.

Inside Terrible Tilly there is a steep spiral staircase. Reportedly, some of the lighthouse keepers would hear a ghostly cry when climbing it.

Terrrible Tilly

Ghost of a Mansion

Isle of Wight, England

Countless generations have lived and died on this small diamond-shaped island—and many residents have claimed to have seen ghosts. If asked, they might say that the spookiest spot on the island is an overgrown field where a mansion once stood.

Isle of Wight

An illustration of the mansion

The 800-year history of the mansion known as Knighton Gorges is filled with bloodshed and misery. In 1170, it served as the hideout for Hugh de Morville, a knight who was said to have murdered the **Archbishop** of Canterbury. Later, in 1721, owner Tristram Dillington lost his wife and children to smallpox. Heartbroken, he drowned himself in the mansion's lake. Now he is said to ride on ghostly horseback through the grounds.

George Maurice Bisset, the owner in 1821, was very displeased with the man his daughter had chosen to marry. In his anger, he had the mansion destroyed. That way, his daughter could never inherit it.

Today, all that is left of Knighton Gorges are some gateposts. Yet the house is said to return at times. How can that be? On New Year's Eve in 1915, Ethel C. Hargrove and a friend saw the mansion emerge out of the darkness. A party was in full swing, with music playing and guests arriving. Now each New Year's Eve, people gather at the gateposts and wait for the ghostly mansion to appear.

The gateposts of Knighton Gorges

Another scary spirit on the Isle of Wight is that of woodcutter Micah Morey. Morey killed his grandson in 1737. After he was found guilty, Morey was hanged for his bloody crime. Since then, his restless ghost has been seen near the site of the hanging, carrying a large ax.

Snake Island

Ilha de Queimada Grande, Brazil

Ilha de Queimada Grande, which lies about 30 miles (48 km) off the coast of Brazil, is a tiny island. Yet it is considered one of the most dangerous places on the planet. People are forbidden to set foot on it without permission from the Brazilian Navy. Why? The island is covered with thousands of deadly golden lancehead **vipers**.

Ilha de Queimada Grande

The golden lancehead viper, which can grow up to 46 inches (117 cm) long, is found only on the Brazilian island of Ilha de Queimada Grande. Its **venom** is so deadly that it can kill a person in two hours. Following an attack, the flesh around the snake's bite begins to rot, while the venom quickly shuts down the person's **organs**. According to people who live near the island, an unlucky fisherman discovered that the snake's venom also stops blood from **clotting**. One day while picking bananas, the fisherman was bitten. He was barely able to return to his boat before dying in a pool of blood.

Golden lancehead viper on Ilha de Queimada Grande

Not surprisingly, the snake has no natural enemies. It has adapted to living mostly in trees. There, it hunts birds using its pits, or sensors, to detect its **prey**'s body heat. As it strikes, the viper bites the bird with its venom-filled fangs. It then holds the bird in its mouth until the venom kills it.

Some scientists estimate that there is one snake per every 11 square feet (1 sq m) on the island.

The Stone Giants of Rapa Nui

Easter Island, Chile

Easter Island, also known as Rapa Nui (RAH-puh NOO-ee), is in the middle of nowhere. The nearest country is Chile, which is more than 2,000 miles (3,219 km) away. When Dutch explorers landed on the far-off island almost 300 years ago, they were amazed that more than 2,000 people lived there. Yet that wasn't the biggest surprise waiting on the island.

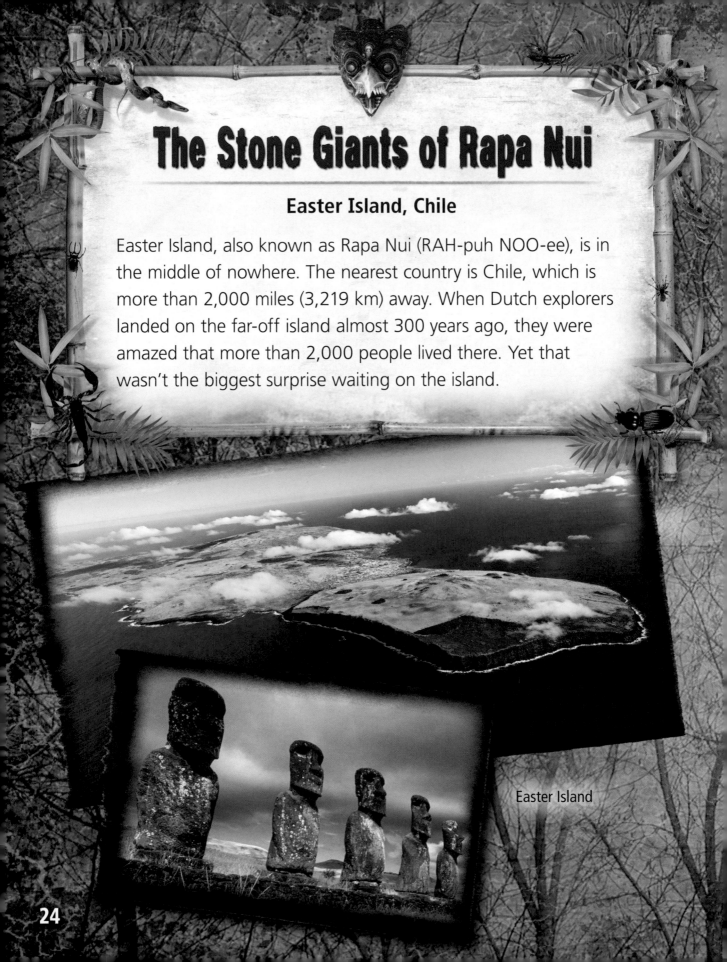

Easter Island

The Dutch first laid eyes on Rapa Nui on Easter Sunday in 1722 and called it Easter Island. Nearly 50 years passed before Europeans visited again. By then, this remote place had become famous throughout the world. People were fascinated by the hundreds of giant stone statues rising up from the ground that the islanders called *moai* (moh-EYE). Carved from hardened volcanic ash, the statues stand, on average, approximately 13 feet (4 m) high and weigh 14 tons (12.7 metric tons). The largest is nearly 72 feet (22 m) high and weighs more than 145 tons (132 metric tons).

A moai

Why were the *moai* made by the islanders hundreds of years ago, and why are there so many? Researchers believe they represent the spirits of ancestors or chiefs. They point out that the *moai* face the sites of the island's old villages, as if they are watching over the people. Researchers are also investigating other questions. For example, why were almost 400 *moai* **abandoned** before they were completed? How were these giant statues moved across the island? With no written records, these mysteries may never be solved.

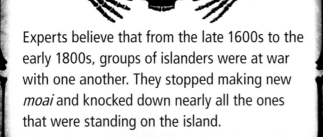

Experts believe that from the late 1600s to the early 1800s, groups of islanders were at war with one another. They stopped making new *moai* and knocked down nearly all the ones that were standing on the island.

Island of the Dead

Hart Island, New York

The island of Manhattan is one of the most crowded places in the world. More than 1.6 million people are packed into just 23 square miles (60 sq km). Nearby Hart Island, however, is actually more crowded—although all of the people on this island are dead.

Hart Island

In 1868, the government of New York City bought mile-long (1.6 km) Hart Island. Officials set aside 45 acres (18 hectares) to be used as a burial ground for people who died with no money or family to claim them. The first person buried there in 1869 was Louisa Van Slyke, who died at age 24 at a New York City hospital for the poor.

Today, prisoners are paid 50 cents an hour to bury the city's dead in large ditches. Each 70-foot-long (21 m) ditch in the cemetery holds between 150 and 165 adult bodies. The wooden coffins, in six rows, are stacked three high. There are separate coffins for body parts. When a trench is full, prisoners cover it with three feet (0.9 m) of dirt and start digging a new one.

Prisoners filling a grave

Because the city's prison department runs the island, no one is allowed to visit the graves. That is rarely a problem, however, since most New Yorkers don't even know Hart Island exists. A small platform at the island's edge is as close as one can get to the graves of the nearly one million people buried there.

Before it became a public cemetery, Hart Island had other uses. At different times, it has been the site of a prison, a hospital, and a training camp for Civil War soldiers.

Deadman Island
Vancouver, Canada

When a visitor arrived here, he found coffins in the trees.

Hart Island
New York

Nearly one million people rest forever on this tiny island.

Appledore Island
New Hampshire

Pirate John Quelch's ghost still searches for his buried treasure.

Tillamook Rock
Oregon

What caused this island's lighthouse to be nicknamed "Terrible Tilly"?

NORTH AMERICA

Roanoke Island
North Carolina

More than one hundred colonists mysteriously disappeared from this island, leaving few clues as to where they might have gone.

Nikumaroro Island
Southwest Pacific Ocean

Did Amelia Earhart crash on this deserted island?

Ocracoke Island
North Carolina

Edward Teach—better known as the pirate Blackbeard— was killed and beheaded off the coast of this island.

Pacific Ocean

SOUTH AMERICA

Easter Island
Chile

Why are there hundreds of giant statues on an island in the middle of nowhere?

Atlantic Ocean

Ilha de Queimada Grande
Brazil

People are forbidden to set foot on this small island filled with poisonous snakes.

Around the World

Arctic
Ocean

EUROPE

ASIA

Isle of Wight
England

This place is haunted by many spirits—and one ghostly mansion.

Ramree Island
Myanmar

During World War II, approximately 900 Japanese soldiers retreated into the jaws of many giant crocodiles.

AFRICA

Indian
Ocean

AUSTRALIA

N

W   E

S

Southern
Ocean

ANTARCTICA

Glossary

abandoned (uh-BAN-duhnd) left alone and uncared for; deserted

archbishop (arch-BISH-uhp) a very high-ranking priest

artifacts (ART-uh-fakts) objects of historical interest made by people

beacon (BEEK-uhn) the light at the top of a lighthouse, used to guide ships at night or during a heavy fog

blockade (blah-KAYD) shutting off an area so others cannot go in or out

clotting (KLOT-ing) thickening or staying in a normally thick liquid state

coffins (KAWF-inz) containers in which dead people are placed for burying

colonists (KOL-uh-nists) people from another country who settle in an area and are ruled by the country from which they came

cove (KOHV) a small sheltered beach

dehydration (dee-hye-DRAY-shuhn) a lack of water in one's body

deserted (di-ZURT-id) having no people living there

isolation (eye-suh-LAY-shuhn) being separate and away from others

legend (LEJ-uhnd) a story handed down from the past that is not always completely true

malaria (muh-LAIR-ee-uh) a disease that comes from the bite of a mosquito and causes chills, fever, sweating, and sometimes death

Native Americans (NAY-tiv uh-MER-uh-kinz) the first people to live in North and South America; they are sometimes called American Indians

navigator (NAV-i-gayt-ur) someone who directs the course that a plane or ship takes

ointment (OINT-muhnt) a thick substance put on skin to heal or protect it

organs (OR-guhnz) parts of the body, such as the lungs or the heart, that do particular jobs

piracy (PYE-ruh-see) robbery that takes place at sea

prey (PRAY) an animal that is hunted and eaten by other animals

remote (ri-MOHT) far away; hard to reach

retreat (ri-TREET) to move away or withdraw from a dangerous situation

settlers (SET-lurz) people who go to live and make their homes in a new place

smallpox (SMAWL-poks) an often deadly disease that causes fevers and painful pimplelike sores that often leave scars

spirit (SPIHR-it) a supernatural creature, such as a ghost

stonemason (STOHN-mayss-uhn) someone who builds with stone

theories (THEER-eez) ways of explaining facts or events

uninhabited (uhn-in-HAB-uh-tid) having no people living there

venom (VEN-uhm) poison

vipers (VYE-purz) certain kinds of poisonous snakes

Bibliography

Austin, Joanne. *Weird Hauntings: True Tales of Ghostly Places.* New York: Sterling (2006).

Hauck, Dennis William. *Haunted Places: The National Directory: Ghostly Abodes, Sacred Sites, UFO Landings, and Other Supernatural Locations.* New York: Penguin Books (2002).

Holzer, Hans. *Ghosts: True Encounters with the World Beyond.* New York: Black Dog & Leventhal (2005).

Wilson, Patty A. *Haunted North Carolina.* Mechanicsburg, PA: Stackpole Books (2009).

Read More

Lewis, J. Patrick. *Blackbeard the Pirate King.* Washington, D.C.: National Geographic Children's Books (2006).

Parvis, Sarah. *Ghost Towns (Scary Places).* New York: Bearport (2008).

Stern, Steven L. *Wretched Ruins (Scary Places).* New York: Bearport (2010).

Yolen, Jane, and Heidi Elisabet Yolen Stemple. *Roanoke: The Lost Colony.* New York: Simon & Schuster Books for Young Readers (2003).

Learn More Online

To learn more about creepy islands, visit
www.bearportpublishing.com/ScaryPlaces

Index

About the Author

Dinah Williams is an editor and children's book author. Her books include *Shocking Seafood; Slithery, Slimy, Scaly Treats; Monstrous Morgues of the Past; Haunted Houses;* and *Spooky Cemeteries*, which won the Children's Choice Award. She lives in Cranford, New Jersey.